Bestul's
Bestuls

Oliver Bestul

Ten|16
PRESS

www.ten16press.com - Waukesha, WI

Bestul's Bestuls
Copyrighted © 2020 Oliver Bestul
Completed in 2017
ISBN 9781645381907
First Edition

Bestul's Bestuls
by Oliver Bestul

For information, please contact:

Ten|16
PRESS

www.ten16press.com
Waukesha, WI

The bestul poem consists of ten lines total, two lines each of ten, eleven, twelve, thirteen, and fourteen syllables. That's a hundred twenty syllables altogether. Those five line pairs can order themselves in any which way, and are not necessarily found as a set of two on the page. For instance, one line of twelve syllables need not immediately follow the other. This poem type generally and loosely rhymes in a pattern like AABBCCDDEE.

Contents

Equinox

The painting had been hailed his finest yet.
An honest depiction of a sunrise had come at last,
which somehow spoke personally to each viewer
as if it were based on a place they once knew or
was otherwise created by their own hand.
That of a young professor inspired protective glass
when she attempted to reach through the gilt frame,
convinced an open window did there hang.
What its artist had decided best to leave unsaid
was the fact that he'd completed the piece while facing west.

Absentee

The violet image she'd penciled consisted
of a great many thin and wavering appendages.
She displayed disappointment in her mother's friend
when he asked whether she'd drawn a lightning strike's random bends.
Her mother's interpretation brought greater distress,
some winter tree's branches, her upside-down guess.
Proximity to the truth can wreck a youthful heart,
and so, in secret, the girl destroyed her art.
In truth, 'twas the roots of their pretty but
sick sycamore, cut down by the city.

Gallery

Among the drawings of objects she'd seen,
tacked onto her wall hung an image from the magazine
that once delivered monthly to her father.
It depicted children huddled together
with limbs like pencils, but bellies like they'd swallowed balloons.
She thought them each similar to cartoons,
or perhaps a photograph she had of her mother,
yellow numbers in the corner days before her birth.
Before she could fall asleep, she had the routine
of giving every stomach a kiss quite gently.

Spiraling

From the cupboard beneath the kitchen sink
she draws a puffy plastic bag of plastic bags, all pink.
Choosing one, she brings it to the backyard without a sound.
One time the trees', helicopter leaves carpet the ground.
Shivering in the fall dawn, she gathers the strange seeds
into a space once claimed by groceries.
Satisfied, she tiptoes her collection upstairs
onto the tiny balcony, moving with care.
Propellers rain from that second floor back porch,
but in vain. Her parents will still get divorced.

I Never Saw a Black Flower Before

Old Missus Klein used to have a tulip garden
that was said to contain twenty-two hundred stems.
People would stop frozen, watching them twist
and swim in the wind. Oh, our mother was envious!
So to cheer her up after Dad left that June,
my sisters and I spent all afternoon
picking each and every single white-maned dandelion
we could find in the field our house stood behind.
Under midnight's cover we snuck amongst those tulips,
blowing away fuzzy seeds. Twenty-two hundred wishes.

Don't Look Down the Middle of the Stairwell

She was only eleven when she said
"I'm never going to be happy again."
They told her she was being dramatic,
but she couldn't hear them over the static
that was pouring across the television's screen,
which reminded her of snow, though snow she'd never seen.
When the other children called her whale, she chewed at her nails,
and in fact was always chewing, so they called her whale.
Writings filled her diary, but they weren't very good.
Nightly she would try to dream, but she never could.

Impressions

She favored movies that showed old photographs
of their star actors, giving the characters a past,
because she figured the quickly-shown pictures all
came from Hollywood homes' mantels and walls,
and she liked the closeness she felt with those on the silver screen
in seeing their families pose, or shots of them as teens,
or other stills of life preceding fame,
as those photos and her own were nearly the same.
Studying the frames on her shelves, she'd remind herself
a time might arrive when she'd be someplace else.

The Only Happy Minutes

Someone pulled the fire alarm this morning.
Everybody awoke to the shrill warning.
We rushed in a line through the halls and outside,
and all would have liked a coat, but had not the time,
so it was she and I in our underwear both.
The early morning wind eroded skin to the bone.
With my palm to hers I was lead towards the bus stop,
clever girl having seen how to avoid the elements.
Thin glass walls of the public shelter we waited behind
until came the time to file back inside.

February and Nearly Sixty Degrees

I found a soundless note while walking around,
blown against the fence that lines the state's fairgrounds.
Blue lettering across a dirty pink paper square
listed the causes of someone's despair.
Forgetting their procedure appointment
got them upset, but they had no one or time to vent.
Without any reason for the marriage, it felt
as though they only wanted to tie someone down.
Perhaps they thought the short tangent through when their words stopped, yet
now I'm left with what they penned sitting in my back pocket.

Shindug

"He told me not to make it a big thing."

"I hope you know that means he wants to feel like a king."

"No, that's not him. He said to take it easy."

"Yes, that's because he's expecting a party."

"It really didn't feel like he was being sarcastic."

"That's just how men get, always talking so drastic."

"So you think I ought to ignore what he told me?"

"I think if you don't, he'll feel as though you're being boring."

When he came home that night to their "Surprise!"

she knew what she had done, seeing the look in his eyes.

Breacher's Once Wife

She had said it was because she was a teacher
that she'd not taken the last name Breacher
when she married the son of a pair of let-down parents,
as it would've so confused her high school students,
but it wasn't that at all. She liked the name.
It was instead because of a boy in the sixth grade
who soon moved away, after he told her
how he'd come back and find her when they were both older.
So she'd kept the same name, but hadn't foreseen
the ways someone can change between adulthood and preteens.

Cats and Dogs

"There are two kinds of girls in the world," his mother would go,
"and it's best if you can avoid them both.
The first, a cat parson and a cat personality,
at home so often you'll question her sanity.
She'll take less love than you're willing to give,
much unlike the dog type, to whom you'll be a sieve
under which she'll sit for any loose bits of rotting
compassion still left in your sunken body.
You'll go broke trying to do all the things she wants to."
"Mom," asked her son, "what kind of person are you?"

Recurrent Elusive Mirage

It's the same dream every night when he hits the pillow case.
At an airport that he's been to before, but can't place,
she sits in such a way that he can't see her face,
but he feels it's her, so his heart starts to race.
In this direction he begins to pace
in slow motion, fighting to move through space.
It's always the same steadfast path that he'll trace,
and, sensing him, she'll start to spin around with grace.
When their eyes meet, he'll awake, as is always the case,
not knowing why he's crying, for his mind has been erased.

Forelock Poor

He was the last person to ever visit the town's mall.
Because he walked the edge of the hall, against the wall,
each shop's sliding glass doors opened up as he passed.
Only teenaged cashiers were there to notice.
His destination, the empty food court
where he first laid eyes on the pretzel girl.
For weeks his dinners had consisted of twisted bread.
This evening he planned to leave nothing unsaid,
but as he neared the counter, he found it closed down.
Instead, he bought a yellow gumball on his slow way out.

No Diving

Our public gymnasium's pool has a lifeguard
who fills up for gas using his parents' credit card,
but only about once or twice a month,
as he can walk to work and class, so never drives a lot.
On his stout tower sits a radio
that was gifted to him by the aunt who once let him know
the truth behind the elusive tooth fairy.
He uses it to play tapes from the library.
Lately the swimmers have listened to Learn French
for the trip to Paris that he's promised his girlfriend.

Several Deadbolts

On Sunday mornings he'd go for a drive
through the neighborhood that stretched along the lakeside
so he could pretend to live in a mansion
between this castle and those palaces
instead of an apartment above a shoe store
with a small hole through the middle of his door
where there was once a lens to look into the hallway
and see the distorted features of anyone knocking
or spy on passersby when their approach was announced
by the floorboards cut from lumber grown in his own hometown.

Bombshell

Now's the time, July ninth, even the date sounded perfect.
For a month he'd been waiting for the right time to surface.
When she was away, he'd gone out and found a ring.
He could hardly wait to watch her wear the thing.
Her folks had smiled and cried when he'd asked for their blessing.
His brother, too, had borrowed him a suit to dress in,
so he fit in good where he took her to eat.
Their talk paused now, she shifted in her seat,
but as his pocketed fingers found the gold band,
he felt he didn't even want her hand.

Repent

On the afternoons he knew his uncle would visit,
he'd reinstall a plywood ramp over the front few steps
which, on that particular day, gave him a thin splinter
in the middle digit of his index finger.
Without the patience or small tongs to operate,
a layer of skin was allowed to heal over it
and there develop a little red bump
that he'd pick at with the nail of his thumb.
When the pastor told them to do what they should,
his thoughts were drawn back to the sliver of wood.

Not Mendocino

She had hoped this trip would be romantic,
digging their feet into a beach on the Atlantic.
What better way to show her devotion
than an all-expense-paid resort on the ocean?
But because her companion hadn't been specific
and explained his longing for the Pacific,
neither of them survived those nights. For the first time,
the sea levels refused to rise from low tide,
instead beginning a decent towards the planet's core,
so that, with her second husband, she explored the sea's floor.

Out of Breath for Nephew

"Why can't we see Aunt Michelle anymore?"
"She and I decided to get a divorce."
"I don't understand why people do that."
"The fast folks slow down. They lose old hair and find new fat."
"Are looks the only reason everyone gets married?"
What could he say to make his sister's kid happy?
"You neglect the turtledoves and misplace all the passion,
fall out of love when she falls out of fashion."
"That's why you two divided?" The boy thought of them as cells.
"No," he hesitated, "ours was for something else."

Lona

But there was Lona! He had her at least.
She had told him of her love when they were each nearly teens.
That was more than half his life ago, but perhaps
if he looked her number up and called, she'd see him again.
Yes! Over coffee, maybe, they'd catch up awhile.
She'd say she'd never married or had a child
or even been on a date since the sixth grade,
denying herself all love but that which they had made.
Surely! They would never part, and would someday own a
home, and throw no stones, and roam. Oh, Lona!

The Most Beautiful Woman

She took her tea overbrewed and bitter,
felt envy when her husband spoke with the babysitter,
sent waitresses back when a sesame was out of place,
only went to games if she could sit behind home plate,
taught her first daughter to eat less than what she needed,
read over receipts to see if she'd been cheated,
screamed if a single hair was found in the shower,
walked out when a movie was more than two hours,
watched mice move in their traps if they'd stayed alive,
and cried herself to sleep when night arrived.

The Ugliest Man

Two of the house's shutters had come loose
and would swing freely when the wind came to peruse.
One had been hung to half-frame the kitchen window.
The other belonged to a bedroom on the second floor.
So frequently did they each smack briefly back into place
that the homeowners could read not or think in the space.
In the middle of a windy night, they'd had enough,
grabbed out a ladder, and ripped every one off.
Un-discolored rectangles adorned their nook,
left alone, for they both liked how it looked.

Could You Head Outside?

He returned from the office completely exhausted.
Five o'clock's second wind used to visit. He'd lost it.
Gone were the days of excess energy
spent on dogs and kids, now dead or at university.
A sigh escaped him when the weatherwoman
predicted a rainy week on channel seven.
It felt as though an ant was crawling up his back,
so he reached with a free hand to try and smack
the bug dead, but none was there. It had been
one of those ghostly sensations felt mostly by children.

Ponytail

The girl asked him "What did you do with your life?"
and had him thinking back to his second wife.
She'd given him a son, a broken thumb,
food poisoning, and had made him feel young.
They used to douse all the lights save a single candle,
then wait motionless, holding each other's hands until
their eyes eventually adjusted to the dimness.
Three or four times they'd make love, but would never kiss.
Sunlight now bounced off the girl's phone's face and into his own,
so he squinted and replied that "I don't quite know."

Fishing Gone

I asked that he take me fishing for one final day.
Used to be we'd cast off twice a week, but his age
started slowing down his body and convincing his mind
that it might be dangerous to even go outside.
However, I could still well remember
watching his bobber in all kinds of weather
as it danced nonstop for each beast in the pond.
His wrists would get sore from reeling in all he caught!
When he heard my request, his face looked worn,
forced to explain how he had no energy anymore.

Old Saint Mary

She'd been to only one place with more religious statues
than the chapel where she prayed the Hail Mary now.
It was her great aunt's house, which she visited once
when six or seven whole decades younger.
A puzzle of the Holy Family neared completion
on a card table in the bungalow's den.
After stale coffee cake and watered-down tea,
her fingers dug out a single small piece.
That which displayed most of the face of the Infant Christ
had remained a part of her, and would until she died.

Just Coincidence

From what I was told, no one was supposed to be home.
They kept a safe to which I'd been given the code.
It would have taken ten minutes, had they not decided
to hire a house sitter for a single night.
She probably woke when I broke the back door's glass panel
and reached inside to unlock its handle.
I was in the basement when she started down the steps,
calling out for what must have been the owners' pet.
When a purr came from above her, she froze.
I had to. No one was supposed to be home!

The Fight

Did you hear about it? I mean the fight.
Something not alright happened to Jane last night.
I guess she and Ben were going at it again.
He says he stormed out, how all their conversations end.
So he's halfway out of town, pedal to the metal ground,
but says a sick feeling turned him around.
Heads all the way back there just to check, he said.
Finds the door wide open, their kitchen painted red.
The cops found a small note in her hand, said "ice cream theme"
and you're always humming that jam, so what the heck's that mean?

I Witness

Perhaps he only heard it. Streetlights had been in his eyes,
but the lawyer knew best and asked him to testify.
Most of what he claimed to know he'd instead been told.
He tried to think back over eight months ago.
Again the gunshot sounded through his head.
Then what happened? He watched as the kid fled.
Blurred right past him wearing a red-- Was that right?
Sometimes he could tell, though a little color-blind.
The jacket must have been, red was written in the file.
Once more he studied the mug shot he by now recognized.

Must've Just Been Glass

He swore for the final time that he was innocent,
but offered no resistance when requested to sit.
Instead he stared ahead, his hands in fists
as leather straps were tightened to secure his wrists.
After the preparation, a brief pause for words profound.
His silence was that of a man underground,
so in their place a short passage was read
moments before a thick bag was brought down about his head.
With his last glimpse, causing my stomach to sink,
I swear I saw him look me in the eyes and wink.

Lap

A shoot-an-arrow-and-it-would-stick kind of fog.
From somewhere to his right, the close-by panting of a dog.
Eyes on the grey halo of sidewalk at his feet
ensure he strays not into an unseen street.
Chill left unfelt, though the cold weather shows.
White billows of breath join the mist from his nose.
With each inhale, the odor of crayons, as if still young.
Taste of Abe Lincoln sits upon his tongue.
For back he's doubled not, it causes his mind brief quiz
when again comes the panting, then he knows where he is.

Trace

On the fourth day he found footprints in snow
that laid like a carpet over the meadow,
and so he built a fire beside those impressions,
camping there for three nights more while he made the decision
to follow and see where the steps would lead,
all the while wondering what their presence could mean.
His boots fit neatly into each depression
as they trekked further on, but his chest felt some tension.
Far ahead stood a shadow where the last imprint fell,
immediately recognized by the man as himself.

All-Night Goodbye

With little sleep and plenty coffee, his stomach felt sour.
He was reminded to stay awake for a few more hours.
By the time the sun would rise, she'd be gone.
She couldn't make eye contact when he'd asked for how long.
Again he was assured this would be good for her.
Both of them, in fact, would be better off than they were.
When she came back, their "troubles will be no more,"
something she'd say when asked what it was for.
Part of each of them knew this was all just pretend
and that they'd never see each other again.

Me and Phoebe, We Used to Be Children

I wonder whether my cat remembers
my coming home with your scent that December.
He won't be around forever, he's grown so thin,
and I don't think you ever got the chance to meet him.
It's not often I ponder this sort of thing.
Some would say it no longer matters, I guess I agree.
When I finally found your house today
with the poor mental map that I formed in ninth grade,
the lights were all out, the curtains drawn shut, the front door
larger than I recall. You must not be home anymore.

Any Old Moment Now

I'm supposed to run into you on the street soon.
You said that's how we'd meet again our last afternoon.
"I promise," you promised, "before we both die,
to find you one final time in this city sunshine."
Well it's been a long life spent waiting on Fortune.
She's never yet nodded, though I know the day approaches,
hopefully while I still have the energy
it would take to embrace you properly.
You're a girl of your word, and always were.
For the first time in years, these ears will hear "Hello, Lover."

In Waiting

Out of the blue, he remembered an afternoon
that he'd spent with his great uncle at the county zoo.
He must have been four or five at the time,
so the old man had a couple-- maybe three years to die.
Neither of them could walk much at their ages,
or stand for too long before each of the cages.
Having discovered a bench, they took a seat
facing the habitat of a dozen small monkeys.
In an hour his mother would retrieve them.
The long minutes until were spent in relative silence.

Getting to Know You

Oh how she'd come to loathe that frequent question!
Why did anybody care what her daddy did?
Time and again she'd watched as their eyebrows rose
at her recital of the initials CEO,
then the unavoidable follow-up,
a request to specify which business it was.
Her cheeks flushed, she'd provide them with the name
of an especially cheaply-made pen company.
All enthusiasm would drain from the inquisitor.
Because of this, she'd years later lose touch with her father.

Destiny

"for a good time, call destiny" and then seven numbers
obstructed the reflection of a face long sunburned.
Rusty eyebrows bowed in concentration.
After a decision, memorization.
Having washed both face and hands in haste, man left that place
grinning at the in-stride sound of packet change.
Eager footsteps to the nearest phone booth.
A pregnant moment's wait, then came the plaint of girlish youth.
Their voices always varied, their question the same.
She assured another it was really her name.

Namesake

Though she'd been told not to go with her friends to see the show,
she figured that her mother would never have to know.
So they picked her up at the back of the house
and drove to where the band would soon play downtown.
The place was too crowded to check IDs,
allowing them each to buy their own adult drink.
Hers she set on a tall table to dance
while a man added his own ingredient to the can.
Until she stepped outside for some air he would wait.
This was the night she would later say destroyed her brain.

Hesitation Wounds

There's a zebra girl who lives down the road
and used to have pink hair, though now I don't know.
She was on my mind the first time I tasted sex,
on my lips while I called another my girlfriend,
in those drawings I would do to try and entertain you,
through which I was exposed to a new slew of blue nude fools.
No emotion could be found in her skin underground,
so I started feeling sorry, and she liked the sound.
When my brother and I are at a store
with razor blades near checkout, I think of her.

Wonder Where

I could tell that something wasn't quite right that morning.
The clothes she'd worn the day before she was still adorning,
and she grabbed my arm when I went for the tea,
explaining how today she needed some coffee.
She was jittery too, as I recall,
eyes darting back to a dot on the wall.
When she turned her head some, I spotted what I fear
was a patch of dried blood behind her left ear.
She got up slow, saying there was someplace she had to be,
and I hear that's the last time the girl was ever seen.

On the Lamb

To see yourself on TV, now that was something,
her beaming senior photo below the red word "MISSING."
An unknown anchor told her she was last seen in Hartford.
That's funny, why hadn't Pete come forward?
She thought they might put her parents on the screen,
but the producers knew those interviews hurt ratings.
Instead they jumped topics to airport security,
then an ad for a condom's durability.
After the distinct sound of an unzip,
a man's hairy hand ripped the tape from her lips.

Couple of Kids

Eleven thirty-one on the digital clock.
They entered without a knock, the door was unlocked.
Music and voices drifted up from downstairs.
They slid into the bed like it was one of the three bears'.
She was nervous below, and he didn't know
whether or not he should sell both their souls.
Had she looked up at him expectantly,
or was she looking to leave and now hesitating?
Only a minute had passed since they'd entered the room.
He noticed the time in the mirror and knew what to do.

Branding

There's a woman on Thursdays and Tuesdays
who makes it hard for men to walk away.
She dances or otherwise stands in the storefront window
while neon has her crown glow with the red kind of halo.
Two pink eyes just behind the shimmering glass
scan over her bated and crimson audience.
Their pulses bulge to the flutter of synthesized songs
about two lovers who decide to die young.
When a number's revealed as her inner thigh moves,
I know she's the little girl I once had to tattoo.

What She Pulls Along

For years she'd been walking that city's streets,
a cart dragged with her, as if she were reverse shopping,
reeking completely and leaving odors behind,
though no one ever paid it any mind.
They all thought her rotting from the inside out,
but she, in fact, smelled alright for someone without a house.
It came instead from the contents of that basket she towed,
under all those milk cartons and old baby's clothes.
In the hit-and-run that claimed her life on ninth and north,
the fact of the matter did come tumbling forth.

Eleanor's Eulogy

Eleanor, you left this place aged only eighty-one,
ending a friendship we'd barely begun.
I took your soft, fragile, little hand in mine,
imagined recognition when you looked into my eyes.
Even as the illness worsened, you seemed so at peace.
Did you see the doves landing at your feet?
If God's responsible for placing you with us,
the Devil placed those lumps inside your head and lungs.
Better to have never loved, as losers paid
when you were gone at eighty-one, just eighty-one short days.

Wrequiem

Every kid in the neighborhood was at that funeral,
mostly because their mothers made them go.
A few black eyes still shined among the audience,
remnants of the boy asleep in his casket,
but they faded after he was buried
alongside the fear their easels once carried.
Something strange then began happening. The beatings
were spoken of as if each was a fond memory.
Instead of "that jerk," the boy was simply called "Jeremy."
By now, only he can recall how it used to be.

J. Gortner

Ugly knots and scars adorning the old tree
make its otherwise too wide trunk ideal for scaling,
so children from the cul-de-sac and beyond
would challenge each other to reach the top.
Only three had reportedly climbed high enough
to see the water tower that stood behind the bluffs.
One was off at college, another my brother,
the third passed away because the juice in his bones went sour.
I always thought if I got up there I'd find his name carved
into the bark, among those knots and scars.

Scrimmage

"Why do you suppose they call them pennies?"

"Maybe it's because they're gold, like coins or money."

"Then what do you say to the reds or blues?"

"I guess I forgot to think about all those."

"Do you think it could be because of what they're paid for?"

"No, I bet shirts and jerseys go for way more."

"But these ones have each got a thousand holes in them."

"That's a good point, but I mean a penny's really not much."

"Yeah. Did you ever flatten any on the train tracks?"

"Why would I-- Oh, you mean pennies? Well sure, of course I have."

Left to Write Wrong

"Dear Mom, Dear Dad, I'm writing from summer camp.
My main complaint is that the weather's been damp,
but, well, I guess there's something else I've been eager
to tell you about, and it's about my cabin leader.
Do you remember Matthew from move-in day? He's the one.
When he's around the other staff, he can be fun.
Other times though, later on, he acts weird,
and I know it costs a lot of dough to send me here,
I just wish you guys could come pick me up.
Love, Dan" said the note Matthew found, and he'd had enough.

Dilapidated

My sister and I would lie in my aunt and uncle's room
at their old house, watching those clay cartoons
and trying to stay away from their Boston terrier,
who terrified us both, every visit scarier!
They later had a hot tub, just inside the fence,
a luxury I've not enjoyed as much since.
Soaking out there with my cousin in the winter,
the spa's plastic rim we'd both lean over
to reach for and pack snow, thrown at a nearby stop sign.
I want to go back there. I won't leave this time.

To Watch It Go

A sound of thunder skirts down along the length of the snake
as its spinal segments click into place.
At an easy pace it begins to slither,
causing that oil in its belly to shiver.
Hissing all the while, the beast increases its speed
and thinks only of catching up to meet
another serpent in the lead, though it never can,
for that creature, too, moves in pursuit of all those ahead.
Only these same winding tracks do they each leave behind.
I'll feed myself to one someday and feel alright.

Dad was on the Train Today

The loneliest souls that walk the good earth
are aging men who like to point out birds
to strangers or their sons while they're on the way
back home, or otherwise headed for yesterday,
and they'll say "how do you do," or perhaps "good morning,"
keeping themselves company, though they'd claim it was for me,
always coughing to clear their throats, it would seem,
for cigarettes they long ago gave up smoking,
maybe wearing a collared shirt and a pair of jeans.
I wish I had a say, but I don't. I see what I'll be.

Nothing Matters to the Tracks

I was sitting two rows from and facing the sliding doors
at the end of my railcar, which led to the next over
and had the same glass panel squarely positioned,
so that one could watch the previous aisle, if one wished.
There stood a man who, in fact, did just that,
staring through both doors' windows, feet from where I sat.
The next car produced its own man, and between
those two sliding doors is where they convened,
speaking for a time before opening them again.
When they returned to their cars, it all began.

Thread Unlimited

Thread Unlimited went out of business quick.
No one who sewed felt as though they needed
additional supplies, and so never stopped by.
Only a single customer ever arrived.
The student had never been to this section
of town, and entered for some direction.
He soon felt so terribly for the aging fellow
behind the counter that he bought a spool of thin yellow.
For flossing, he'd cut a generous length twice a day
until not a tooth remained. The shop had been aptly named.

Shape-Shifting Woman

"Looked up from the magazine ad she's in, and there she was,"
I recall as he holds a photo of us.
Before long, he's opening his eyes wide,
asking to look twice if I'd like to see why.
He points not to her, but to the ground behind us both,
and I'm told to notice a pair of shadows.
The first is mine, with well-defined lines on the cement,
but hers is blurred, as if she stood at a distance.
"Some trick of the lighting," I start to say,
then I realize the reason she'll often touch her face.

Gone, but Forgotten

Just for a moment I say what I feel,
and in a minute those eyes brim with tears.
In an hour I've no one for my arms to help wrap in.
In a day I'm told to forget we ever happened.
In a week I forget what we fought about.
In a month I forget what we'd talk about.
In a year I forget just how that voice used to sound,
and in five I throw away the last letter I found.
In a decade I can't put a name to the face,
and beyond that not even a smile remains.

Our Last

Here's a game the both of us can play. It's named
"What would you do if you knew I planned to die today?"
Should you choose to stay with me tonight, there are a few rules.
The first, if you fall in love with me you lose,
second, show no emotion should we meet after,
and third, never tell anyone else about what happens.
For best results, try to leave nothing undone or said.
After twelve this evening, we never speak again.
You can say no, you're in either way though.
Ready or not, on your mark, get set, go.

A Formal List of All the Things from Jacqueline I Kept:

a formal list of all the things from Jacqueline I kept:
the filter from when I asked to bum a cigarette
coconut lip balm she said gave her a headache
the candle she licked clean from my birthday cake
a stem from the ghost pepper that she tried
a bendy straw she couldn't use for the hole in its side
a little foam wedge with which she blotted her lipstick
an olive pit with a bit of the tooth it chipped
cheap Dracula fangs she wore on Halloween
the memory of her mouthing "please leave"

On a

I thought she'd walk past me, but she paused in front,
having forgiven me for that which I'd done.
Looking up silently, I was brought to my feet
by the delicate hand she'd extended in me.
Mine on her waist, hers moving to my face,
both afraid of this awaited embrace.
Limply, plump lips are at last allowed to meet. As we waltz,
tears for wasted time apart bring my tongue a taste of salt.
Froze without prose for fear of what we might say talking--
but no, this hadn't happened. She'd simply kept walking.

Second Last Morning of First Semester

Abby had said, the night before, we'd catch up in a month.
She'd have a roommate, though, so I'd not visit as oft.
It was Nick's last day here, spending next year at home.
"See you around" to my last friend in the dorm.
Someone still around in the dining hall
looked away, so we never met at all.
Beauty from behind the front desk was I guess
now moving to Europe as another school's guest.
A clot of blood smudged on my otherwise white tee shirt,
but I didn't mind. There was no one around to see it.

First Last Evening of First Semester

Earlier today, I was eating fervently,
knowing that lunch was the last meal they were serving.
Went out and took my last exam, then returned to the cold
of my residence hall, as there was no one else home.
I scrubbed off the message they'd penned on my door
with a dampened sock I'd earlier peeled from the floor.
Having found a dollar, I bought dinner
from a vending machine. It made me feel like a winner.
What's strange is that now I'm in the main lounge
and can, for the first time, hear the background's sounds.

Where Does the Cube Man Go?

It was late January of my second semester.
Our campus experienced record low temperatures,
falling to just above fifty below.
The pipes of the tallest residence hall froze and broke,
displacing its students, so that my building soon
had a cot delivered to each warm dorm room.
Someone must have read Kelly, and in their haste
assumed I was a woman, so they placed
that freshman girl in my company. For those three weeks
we knew each other, then never again did speak.

Ides

His sister's kids never had an aunt or cousins
and were visibly unexcited when they'd visit him.
Here the closest thing to a toy was his aftershave,
which came in a bottle shaped like a fish and had engraved
on a nickel plate the maker's name, Ides,
so he decided to buy, for their sake, a surprise.
When the family next came through his front door,
a kitten was waiting on the hardwood floor,
but because his brother-in-law carried dessert,
he failed to see who his next steps would hurt.

Angel of Pursuit

Every day since he'd gotten her letter
an hour was spent on the park bench where he first met her,
always with a flower in his nervous lap,
which was either picked along the walk from his apartment
or otherwise bought at the corner, during winter months.
He knew not how long he'd been waiting for her to come,
but it was only a week after he received
her note telling him where they were to meet
that she crossed the lake and into the city.
The accident happened walking off that ferry.

Sinking Feeling

His face was pressed against the ceiling now,
eyes wide, like a fish to which water had not been allowed,
whose expression would reflect peace again once submerged,
but for the time being lacked any scrap of courage.
Undersea feet kicked to keep his carcass afloat.
He then remembered the letter she wrote
was in the top drawer of this cabin's desk.
She'd come with him. He sucked thin air into his chest,
dove down, yet found he was missing the small key,
so tried to resurface, but the room had filled completely.

Sibling Revivalry

An un-unique bodyguard blocked the paparazzi
from shooting a movie star who'd dodged all publicity
since the recent passing of her brother.
He likewise had spent time in the limelight when younger.
Their audience once thought them identical
until a few injections sort of changed her look,
and they stopped being cast in the same flicks
with this new lack of a family resemblance.
Yet now they began to look alike once more.
She'd cut all her hair off, and the people needed to know.

Saint Anthony

A windstorm left his skin worn red, since he
had spent the day clearing streets and walkways for the city.
He'd just finished sweeping up rended bark when
his department got a call from an upturned park bench.
It partly blocked the bike path that ran along the lake,
and so they sent him in to investigate.
Because the gust had upside-downed the public seat,
he was able to see something caved underneath.
The etched message read "K.M. loves E.M."
then the date, August twenty-six, nineteen ninety-seven.

Very Ugly Necklace

Sifting through and trying on her mother's jewelry box,
she came upon a nude man lying on a silver cross
who seemed out of place among gold chains with fake gemstones.
The only little person there, he must feel alone.
There was something funny about how his head hung,
as if he was afraid of whoever he'd hug,
and his feet looked like hers practicing ballet,
but that's not something she'd ever done naked!
Suddenly, he seemed like a small monster,
so she left him, as had done her mother.

Hummingbird

She'd train her eyes on the Great Lake's horizon,
once each morning, once at night, when the ferries came in,
for her brother had told her their mother now lived
at the bottommost point of Michigan.
Studying every new batch of businessmen
as they drove or strolled away from the docking station,
the longed-for moment of their reunion
had, for seven years, been patiently awaited.
Now was the summer when she'd at last come to understand
how Mom had gotten where she was by way of the Hoan Bridge.

Now's Your Chance

Walking along the beach, she'd tripped on the embossed
handle to a lamp she ran a single finger across.
The thinnest mist spouted out of its tip,
and a reedy voice begged her for a wish.
She stood there, frozen in anticipation or fear,
reminded of blowing out candles each year,
or thumbing her loose change into a fountain,
like spotting meteors while hiking around mountains.
Now came that familiar sense of feeling lost,
having gone through life not knowing what she wanted at all.

She Liked My Name

There was something about the way you looked at me that day
that seemed to tell me what you otherwise couldn't say.
As you hung on every lungful I tongued up
and giggled at my unfunny jokes, I thought I saw
a type of fire burning beneath your clothes and skin.
I was in love for a lingering moment then.
Were you not also? Yes! I saw it there!
Electricity straightening your arm hair.
But you stopped me when I began to speak
to remind me that you'd not be here by this time next week.

I Didn't Try to Objectify

She got off at Winona and shared my cousin's name.
I was starting to like her. She was starting spring break.
Her major was woman studies, law school was coming next,
but she'd not become a lawyer like her parents.
Born in Chicago, she now went to school there.
Once bored with her book, she'd made fine conversation,
but before we'd begun talking, she'd adjusted her tights.
Closing my eyes, I memorized the sight
of the hand between her thighs, groping fabric
for only a brief yet damning second.

After All

The last person to see her face when it was beautiful
was a new, teenaged driver whose view was pulled
from the road when he heard his phone's ringtone,
and so checked to see if there was any news from home,
as his brother had stopped saying he was alright.
A high tolerance for pain had given the cancer time
to bloom. It was too late to take any action.
For this, he drove distracted through the intersection.
She had been on the way to her first date
with a sad doctor who left when she was late.

Pinprick

Erica was then in training to be a tour guide.
She'd always loved caves, and so she'd applied.
The test on rock formations she'd passed with flying colors.
Her kindly demeanor, too, surpassed all the others.
Took her deep inside the mountain, the last task on the list,
and they cut the lights, as they would for a tourist.
Just black she thought she saw, until she realized
a speck of silver light sat before her eyes.
When she mentioned it, as the team ate their lunch,
everyone got real quiet all at once.

Killing Time

Having arrived early, from his pocket he quietly
removed a plastic egg of inedible taffy.
Standing in the dim-lit room's dead center,
he rolled between his palms a small ball from the tender
dollop he'd gotten when only a kid.
Pinching some between his free index and thumb, he twisted
and did so until he held a type of spiral
that looked to him like a tongue-colored tornado.
Upon hearing the alarm's beep from his wrist,
the toy he put away, then shot she who slept.

Run for Your Lives

He held his breath during this final step.
For stability, he pinned his elbows against his chest.
His head he brought slightly back from the pair of small pieces.
Holding them both so close, his eyes had lost focus.
That in his left hand he rotated but a fraction
of a minute clockwise, so they both sat matching
and aligned, as if divine fingers had so guided
those that were his own. The components glided
together into one, and his lips curled,
for he had brought about the end of the world.

And so They Tried

Shouldering open his door, he stumbled to the mattress.
In thirty seconds more, they'd be making their arrest.
He reached underneath and into the box spring,
but fingered only hanging tape where he'd placed the thing.
Finding nothing on the floor below caused him to panic
and ask aloud "Who could've known that I had it?"
Boots pounding down the hallway called to mind
the pistol he kept belted to his side.
Their foremost soldier never fired a single shell,
because he brought justice down upon himself.

Army Man

Beneath the boy's bed, there sat an old tin lunch box
that he liked to drag out when he had his bedroom door locked.
A tiny green battalion scattered within,
each brave man lying poised with his own plastic weapon.
With great care he'd arrange them on his bedside tabletop
in a semicircle and aiming at the same spot.
Crouching down some, he'd be at eye level.
His blood would pump fast then, like he'd seen a devil.
The squad's sights all trained on his trembling head,
he'd wonder aloud why his brother was dead.

America's Pastime

It had become clear which was the better team.
A seven-run lead, bottom of the final inning.
With two outs, this would be the last at-bat of the season.
Our worst hitter walked to the plate with a cheek of seeds and
their three outfielders took a dozen steps forward.
No one saw his eyes, as his helmet was lowered,
but the grin he had on I can still well remember.
At the first strike, he ran to the pitcher
and kept his stick swinging at the boy's face.
When the third base coach stopped him, it was too late.

Biding

For lack of a better course of action
he found himself listing increasingly slight fractions,
which simply entailed adding to the denominator
in increments of one, maintaining his numerator,
seeing more clearly with each number he wrote
the lonely top digit, a girl on a thin boat
sailing away on an ever-growing ocean
that had, by now, become the man's only devotion,
and so a second sea he began to bawl
when he ran out of space on the brick walls.

Free at Last

The mattress had been sold and replaced with a plywood board.
All carpeting had been torn from the floor.
Though winter, the heater was not put to use.
Walls were stripped, including the drawing of Zeus.
Furniture, too, was dealt out to old friends.
Fluorescent lightbulbs screwed in place of those with filaments.
Only frozen food was not entirely refused.
A tin bucket in the corner served as the restroom.
Vertical stripes of paint were on the windows as well.
They'd kept his room the same, but he needed his cell.

Con's Pro

A man said "I'll show you the rest of your life, one nickel."
I forked over the coin, wasn't the time to be fickle.
He said "Do you want the good news or the bad news first?"
I said "Well, sir, I guess you ought to start with the worst."
I'd never seen such tears and blood in all my days.
I'll outlive all my kin, then they'll send me away.
My next few words must've sounded like whining.
I asked the man for any silver lining.
He said "Well, son, you'll have all those sad tunes
stretched over the next baker's dozen moons."

Confessional

Forgive me, Father, for I'm a sinner.
What all I have done has turned me thinner.
Twin hollows, which now cradle my eyes, do tell
that I've seen certain scenes sure to seat me in Hell.
Teeth, having grown long, chatter always solely
to display how I've eaten meats most unholy.
Hands with knuckles rubbed bare sit as fists as if to show you
the variety of things I've held, but wasn't meant to.
I fear all the angels and saints will dismember me.
After which, only Lucifer will remember me.

Jacob's Seesaw

When she said she needed me, I knew she was wrong.
She only saw my brother, but I played along.
Because she was able to get the clothes he died in,
I was assigned that uniform, and blindly abided.
He was hooked up to oxygen at the end,
so she had me wear a breathing tube, just for pretend.
Apparently, he would sing to her while she was unclothed.
At her insistence, I performed this role.
What, then, could surprise after all of this?
The pain that I, like that brave man, did inflict.

The Fox-Trot

We've just received some breaking news from a southside dog park
where a hostage situation has developed.
A man and three highly trained German shepherds
have corralled every pet to the grass lot's center.
Of the dozen distraught owners, none have been allowed near.
One woman has reportedly broken into tears
after her attempt to call back a goldendoodle
that was swiftly bit at the neck and killed.
Our sources tell us over the crowd's shouts--
Oh God, he's actually stomping them out!

Padded Lockbox

There would be these brief blips of lucidity
during which he was made able to more clearly see
his own whereabouts, and he began to understand
that he had perished, but had not been damned!
By some mistake, he'd found the narrow gate
and had been allowed to take someone else's place
at the feast where angels garbed white bring nourishment
to the lips of those in this bright, controlled establishment.
While somehow assigned cloud nine, with its six massive panels,
he'd flip most of the time through his mind's annals.

Patient

When showed a photograph of an electric power plant,
a spike in activity flooded his brain scan.
Eye-tracking sensors indicated fixations
on individual rivets, intersecting shapes, then
the bottom of a cloud in the background.
Reviewing his heart monitor charts, we found
that a quickened pulse coincided with this
prolonged observation of the cumulonimbus,
yet lie detector testing verified
his immediate claims of forgetting the white sight.

The Royal Blue

The king was instrumental in maintaining global peace,
admired by each ambassador he'd meet
and regarded as the epitome of virtue,
for of his beloved concubine, none knew.
When a fever gradually ceased her breathing,
only he and the priest came to see her buried.
This public's indifference he learned to rue,
so had repaired the rifle his grandfather once used.
He awaited the hour his queen found sleep
to bite down and tongue its barrel. Now the whole world would weep.

Badlands

"For he who is reading this, all hope is lost.
Eternal damnation is all that awaits us.
A house was once erected in this place
and placed in the hands of those assumed virtuous and chaste,
but who have laid it at the feet of they who weep
in the face of an impending and everlasting heat.
Man shall never know of that garden again,
instead condemned to forever endeavor. Amen."
Signed and dated by a priest long dead, found
within the hollow cornerstone of a church now downed.

To Bleach

"Genetic hiccups," a phrase I'll not forget,
used by teacher in describing statewide eugenics.
She asked us "Whose families celebrate Saint Patrick's Day?"
Those whose hands rose were escorted away.
Then she held out government-issued skin color swatches
to compare to pale stripes under each of our watches.
Children with more melanin were likewise removed,
until only six of us remained in the room.
We all had foil stars stuck onto our charts
and began a lesson on the human heart.

Stucco

"Lead content: fifty-three parts per million.
Mercury content: twenty parts per billion.
Arsenic content: seven--" The machine was switched off,
its thin, sterile probe removed from the glass of water.
Orange light shone through the open doors to the veranda
from the midnight sky, inciting him to wonder
whether there was ever truly a time
when more than just the dim moon could be seen to shine.
Attempting to quench what thirst he'd never know,
he tilted back his head and poured the liquid down his throat.

Ripples

My daughter was killed for a twenty-dollar bill
on a shortcut she took to get home to her children.
Three boys stepped in front of her car at a stop
in a part of town that sees the police a lot.
A pistol was held five inches from her head
by he who sought something priceless, destroying it instead.
The gunman was just twenty-one years old,
and reached over her body to grab cash for his smokes.
Because I wasn't able to save her,
when he's released in thirty years I'll repay the favor.

There Are Things Worse Than That

Look not upon these eyes, I fear they may betray
all the thoughts that I've been having today.
What's worse than an unthinking criminal of passion
is one with unblinking fantasies who hasn't acted,
for the soul of the former stays untouched in a way,
while that of the latter is subject to decay.
Better when I cut the legs from that spider
than now, when I think I could have used fire.
Yesterday I would have hanged, today they should be suing
for the many odd things I've thought of doing.

Nothing's Going to Happen to Us

Nobody remembered to tell him it was getting cold,
so he had no way of knowing it was time for a coat.
He stood fixed before the windows of a closed-down store,
dreaming of the day he'd not shop anymore.
A small girl looked upon his bare back and wept
until her mother listed all the places he'd been.
Someone else noticed his whispering lips
and began the people wondering what they dripped.
Dared by three friends, a woman approached and leaned in
to hear the name he'd always repeated.

Sound

He perked up his head when he heard the noise,
something he'd not heard since he was a boy, another's voice.
It reverberated from the mouth of his cave,
where the light came in and he'd not been for a decade.
The words that had been spoken he know not.
A language that was once his had been forgot.
In an attempted reply, outpoured a shallow exhale.
For a lack of use, his vocal cords had failed.
To communicate instead, he pounded the ground.
His visitor fled, knowing the danger they had found.

More Ornate Lately

That was the last of it. Even the droplets
on his chin from the goblet's rim had been licked
into his grinning lips by a fat tongue.
Seven seconds later, he coughed up the air of his lungs.
His eyes then did bulge above a nose now bleeding
and between ears deaf to all but a certain ringing.
Both hands groped over the table, his right finding the knife
he sheathed through the temple, ending all life.
The only hound allowed lapped at a growing puddle
underneath the body that began to dissolve.

Liver Dye

No one can know one another in another life.
Doorman or niece, your memories will die,
be they wrought in steel, or other rotten coppers,
so no use seeking fuse watts or other sinking waters.
Save sailing, the seven seas don't seem so sweet.
Don't be seen afraid of raids of busy bees.
The alcohol has called them all away,
a way to save all the wise dames who would otherwise pay.
Were the world the germs' or all the worms', your journal
would fall the first of all the worst attempts eternal.

Stop It

Jack would say "I'm sorry" over and over when alone.
He felt as though he meant it, though for what he didn't know.
Tom had started at the job they all said he'd like.
They'd never been right before, but he'd give it a try.
Al's crossword showed that his mind had started to go.
It sat before him blank for the fifth day in a row.
Susan squinted at and old photograph,
recognizing all but a man in the back.
Jan set the supper table up just so,
but no one ate. She'd had the oven too low.

Another Unborn Mourns Their Day

Because they'd decided not to have kids,
a son who was supposed to grow up never did,
and so couldn't someday hit the dog of a ten-year-old
who, unbrokenhearted, needed nothing to be consoled.
When her father had no reason to buy her ice cream,
he also had no chance to spit his gum in the street,
which, in turn, did not stick itself to the shoe
of a girl on her way to the last day of school.
Had she the excuse for pausing in the hall
to peel it off, she and Dad would've talked.

Smudge

There's a smudge at the edge of the page, and how.
Not always was there, but so is there now.
Erase and white paint it, if time does so allow.
Bleach, burn, and tear 'til there's sweat on your brow.
Yet still it does thrive, as unmoved as a sterile sow.
Indeed, without vitality, the thinnest, milkless cow.
A resilience that comes with the power to wow.
That chases away companions and a marital vow.
And leaves those it touches without breath to say ow.
There's a smudge at the edge of the page, and how.

Though

There was something in the back of his head
that could hold him to the pillow, as if made of lead,
and would bring his gaze skywards in lamentation
when his neck was forced back with the heavy sensation.
At other times, though, one might call its weight light,
sending him soaring out into the middle of the night
or laughing at himself to the point of no breath,
a gaiety that seemed without chance of death.
No matter what he attempted to do,
the thing was there in its lair under his hair and he knew.

Through a Thin Skin

She had stopped peering up for the stars at night
as they looked about the same as faraway streetlights,
and those she could take in without craning her neck.
Buds plugged her ears when to the beach she trekked,
playing seaside sound effects into twin canals
because she felt as though real seagulls sounded too frail.
In too much pricy perfume she'd soak her clothes,
the only scent she needed in her nose
when traveling the streets of the city in which she lived.
Her mother would wonder if she'd been this way as a kid.

Decellularized

A lonely only known to him alone
who'd never sent a ten-second photo,
or made faces at a girl with just his thumbs,
or expressed any liking without his lungs.
Their marrow baked brittle by backlit telephone screens
as cold to him as the ides of February,
for he'd never felt the warmth of picture instancy,
his character unconfined to a hundred and forty.
Having not swiped right, he had no wife there at his side
when, on death's doorstep, he wept for all the unwasted time.

Except After C

The tie that he wore clipped onto his collar.
He used to knot the real deal, but no longer bothered.
On his bus sat the would-be train passengers who'd not guessed
that an avalanche might cover the tracks out west.
At the station, they had each been checked in.
My own name was included on that list.
While riding through the landscapes of bitter trees and shacks,
I stood to use the restroom located in the back.
A girl I failed to recognize watched from my reflection.
We drove over a terrible pothole then.

qiū tiān

"Your next sleep will be a permanent one."
On the back, "Learn Chinese," the word for autumn.
As he swallowed the cookie from Minghao Express,
it was certain by tomorrow in peace he would rest.
He dialed the number of his third-best ex-girlfriend, Jeanne.
The first two had let it go to their answering machines.
He told her he loved her and missed lying on her chest.
She calmly convinced him that he needed some rest.
For the very first time, once under the sheets,
he had no problem in falling asleep.

Canyon Echoes

That last note simply read "I couldn't wait any longer."
Folks in town all got to thinking what they'd done to wrong her.
She'd been unheard all along, so it hardly made sense
how now that she was gone, she should find her audience,
but those five words, they found their way to every ear.
Alone at night, tykes would recite them out of fear.
Everywhere was the phrase spray-painted in blue,
including highway signs to greet passers-through,
even tattooed onto the chief's daughter,
in a spot, though, where he never caught her.

Outdated Security Cameras

This city had a certain smell at night
once everyone was done pretending things were alright,
like a strange mixture of fake banana candies
and a hand after filling up on gasoline.
Charcoals were doused, sidewalk chalk was left out,
a thousand pill bugs made love under each house.
The mailman stayed awake late on Saturdays
to bake an always uneaten vanilla bean cake.
He used his son's final note to collect dust on the shelf.
"Dear Dad, I don't like you as much as I dislike myself."

Tycoon

A man called Alfred Stork once found some oil underground.
Now his name adorned a plaza that sat downtown.
It was etched neatly into a slab of rock
and stood four feet above the public sidewalk,
each letter seven inches tall and a half an inch deep.
The stonemason responsible had died in his sleep.
Like an inlaid shelf the T's top was used
to hold a sucker stick, some candy still infused.
Stork always said "black gold can go rotten,"
but no one wrote the words down, and so they were forgotten.

Hand Me Down

The last Adolf died today in New Berlin, Wisconsin,
born in nineteen eighty-nine to a pair of immigrants
who wanted their son to fit in, and so found his name
in a list of those who brought America great change.
He became very good at playing solitaire
at a young age, and often read books on childcare,
though he had no children, nor had he married
by the time no one came to see him buried.
One hundred and seven was the man's age
when he left the world in a fit of rage.

Moe

He'd been a surgeon first, then an immigrant,
then our city's only honest mechanic.
With the purposeful use of his two steady hands,
every job he was given was finished in minutes.
I can still remember the morning when
the keys were slid back to me and my dad
and we started walking to the newly-repaired car.
This third man followed us both out of the garage.
Some minute detail was remembered, which he'd not explained.
Behind where he stood simply waved his brand-new country's flag.

Signal

The phrase "Keep Tobacco Sacred" had been painted
below the face of a woman recently sainted
on a mural that ran along the walls
surrounding a garden in downtown Kinnickinnic Falls.
Escorting his grandfather along the path,
a young man watched me wash my face in the birdbath.
When they were both upon me, the grandson spoke.
"Hey, bro." I straightened up. "Throw me a smoke?"
When my index and thumb met, this hand became okay.
I told him "got none," and the pair went on their lonely way.

Mile Seven

A hawk perched just outside the classroom window
as a native man taught us to tap syrup from maples.
When it looked into me, I stopped listening.
Our speaker, with two braids in, started hesitating.
The handshake he gave me after his words
was on my mind still while walking down to dinner.
I sat just across the table from her.
Both of us spoke of our own significant others.
On leaving, I was told to give mine a big kiss.
My reply was that I'd do so for her, and I meant it.

Thou Shalt Not

Oh let this rubber sleeve stretch thin and rip!
Of her daily medicine I beg a malfunction.
Leave me not to carry on as always planned.
As always, planning brings about my line's sterile death.
Like a thousand beasts before me, I've learned to sow,
but none before have ceased their own seeds' growth.
None before have known the feeling of alone
that awaits me in my home of ringing echoes.
With the springtime's end must come this young passion's conclusion,
unless an escape is made to occur between our hips.

A Nigher End Than We Can Pretend

Far back into his refrigerator's freezer
he found a gallon drum of ice cream set to expire
tonight, the twenty-second of the month.
No one came to mind that he could share it with,
so a single spoon and bowl were removed
from the place he liked to store his bowls and spoons.
At the kitchen table he sat down and began
to attack the great amount of dessert that he had,
but his stomach soon cramped. With a burning heart he gave up
and decided instead to throw the whole container out.

Bachelor Again

He woke tired still, having dreamt a span of several days
over the course of a single night. Through the haze
in his head he could remember a few brief episodes
from the entire imagined week or so.
So bluntly she'd confessed to having an affair!
Then came the finding of her in another man's lair.
The worst and most vivid image with him now,
though, was the hallway he'd watched her walk down,
because he understood as their distance grew
that no woman had the power to keep him enthused.

The Music of Anything But

I left a concert hall today before the first band played.
It may or not have been the best decision ever made.
A petty game of cards was lost, my attendance
was all I had to bet, and so I went,
but upon sitting down, I decided
that one more classical tune would cause me to cry
bitter tears for the long minutes of my life gone lost.
Instead, I'll sit on this park bench watching moss
and ignoring the sun that sets behind me
for attention. This Mississippi is exhausting.

Virgin Swan Song

With careful watercolors, she'd only paint squares.
Plant matter would find itself in her hair.
When spoken over, she became sensitive,
especially after nights where she'd dream of him.
Drinking from a canning jar, making love on the floor,
shaking in the bus stop rain, leaving a crack in her door.
Balloons taped to her ceiling, a tattoo for each heartache,
apple sanitizer, that gazebo on the lake.
She knew the origin of everything green,
and would call herself uninteresting.

Pine

Needles cover the forest floor, but not of evergreens.
These are man- or machine-made, each with a polished sheen.
Reaching down to collect, one enters my slender finger
and passes through as if it were made of soft butter.
Pierced, I falter and fall to the carpet
of thin pins even longer and sharper yet.
My person greets an unholy acupuncture,
calling back a face to my brain's creased junctions.
Though the quills' sting concocts a bodily tonic,
none smart as lovely as Veronica.

www.ingramcontent.com/pod-product-compliance
Lightning Source LLC
Chambersburg PA
CBHW070810050426
42452CB00011B/1980